Date: 5/28/19

Working in SPACE

by Ellen Lawrence

Consultant:
Josh Barker
Space Communications Team
National Space Centre
Leicester, United Kingdom

BEARPORT
PUBLISHING

New York, New York

Credits

Cover, © NASA; 4, © ESA/NASA; 5, © NASA; 6, © ESA/NASA; 7, © NASA/Crew of STS-132; 8, © NASA; 9, © NASA; 10T, © NASA; 10B, © Nipaporn Panyacharoen/Shutterstock; 11, © NASA; 12T, © Vlad G/Shutterstock; 12B, © Henrik Dolle/Shutterstock; 13, © NASA Photo/Alamy; 14, © ESA; 15, © ESA/NASA; 16, © ESA/Getty Images; 17, © NASA; 18, © NASA; 19, © NASA; 20, © NASA; 21, © NASA; 22CL, © ravl/Shutterstock; 22BL, © ScriptX/Shutterstock; 22R, © Sean Locke Photography/Shutterstock; 23TL, © NASA; 23TC, © Kateryna Kon/Shutterstock; 23TR, © Bullstar/Shutterstock; 23BL, © NASA/Victor Zelentsov; 23BC, © Denis Tabler/Shutterstock; 23BR, © NASA.

Publisher: Kenn Goin
Senior Editor: Joyce Tavolacci
Creative Director: Spencer Brinker
Photo Researcher: Ruth Owen Books

Library of Congress Cataloging-in-Publication Data

Names: Lawrence, Ellen, 1967– author.
Title: Working in space / by Ellen Lawrence.
Description: New York, New York : Bearport Publishing, [2019] | Series:
  Space-ology | Includes bibliographical references
  and index.
Identifiers: LCCN 2018050771 (print) | LCCN 2018052256 (ebook) | ISBN
  9781642802450 (ebook) | ISBN 9781642801767 (library)
Subjects: LCSH: Manned space flight—Juvenile literature. | Space
  environment—Juvenile literature. | Life support systems (Space
  environment)—Juvenile literature. | Space stations—Juvenile literature.
  | Space vehicles—Juvenile literature. | Astronauts—Juvenile literature.
  | Outer space—Exploration—Juvenile literature.
Classification: LCC TL793 (ebook) | LCC TL793 .L29948 2019 (print) | DDC
  629.45—dc23
LC record available at https://lccn.loc.gov/2018050771

For more information, write to Bearport Publishing Company, Inc., 45 West 21st Street, Suite 3B, New York, New York 10010. Printed in the United States of America.

10 9 8 7 6 5 4 3 2

Contents

Time for Work!

An astronaut on the International Space Station (ISS) puts on a spacesuit.

He grabs some tools and clips on ropelike safety tethers.

A door opens, leading to the blackness of space.

It's time for the astronaut to go on a space walk!

an astronaut getting ready for a space walk

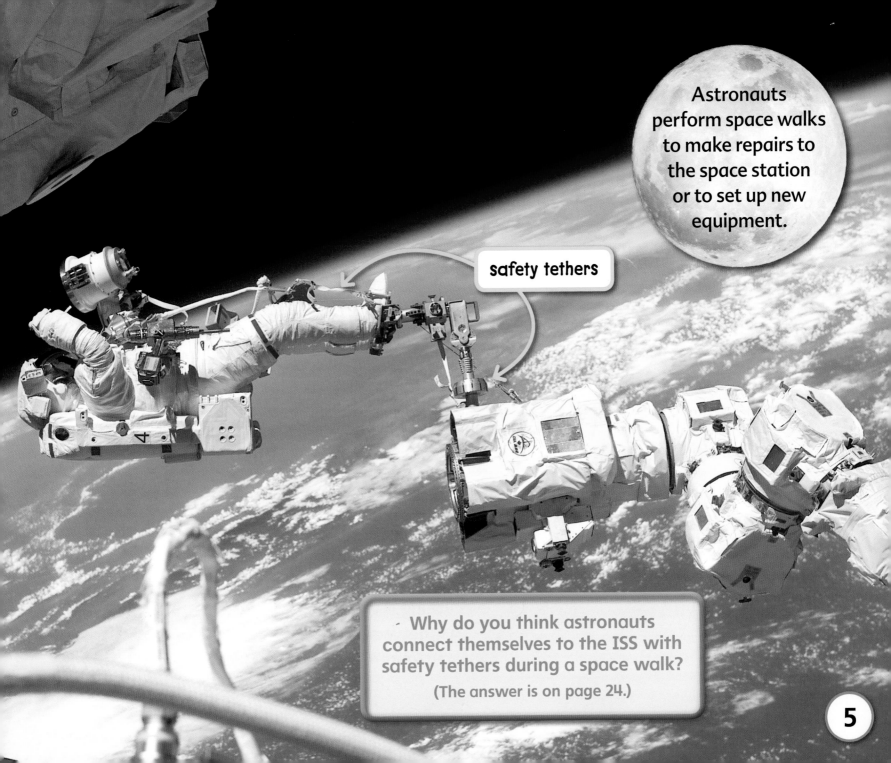

Astronauts perform space walks to make repairs to the space station or to set up new equipment.

safety tethers

Why do you think astronauts connect themselves to the ISS with safety tethers during a space walk?

(The answer is on page 24.)

5

A Flying Laboratory

The ISS is a big **laboratory** that's **orbiting** the Earth.

Onboard, a crew of six astronauts performs science experiments.

The space station has three main laboratory areas, or modules.

Each module is about the size of a school bus.

At any time, the crew may be working on 150 different experiments!

On Earth, everything is pulled toward the ground by gravity. In space, everything is weightless. As they work, the astronauts are floating!

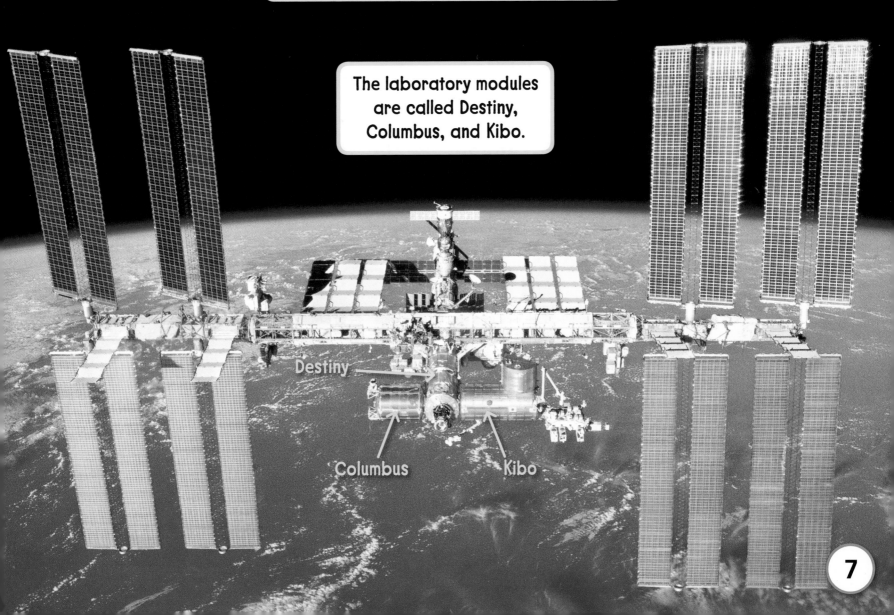

The ISS is about 250 miles (402 km) above Earth's surface. It's moving through space at almost 5 miles per second (8 km/s).

The laboratory modules are called Destiny, Columbus, and Kibo.

Destiny

Columbus

Kibo

Human Experiments

The ISS astronauts also carry out experiments on themselves. Why?

Scientists want to know how being in space affects the human body.

American astronaut Scott Kelly lived on the ISS for 340 days.

He carried out hundreds of tests on his body before, during, and after his **mission**.

Scott Kelly performing tests on his body

Scott Kelly's identical twin brother, Mark, also took part in the experiments. Mark stayed on Earth and did the same tests as Scott. This allowed scientists to compare the results.

Scott Kelly's Mission

- Monitored every part of his body, including his eyes, heart, bones, and muscles
- Studied how his blood was affected by weightlessness
- Investigated how well his body could fight off illness in space
- Collected samples of his own blood, spit, pee, and poop to be studied back on Earth

Mark (above) and Scott giving themselves flu shots

9

Space Gardens

One day, astronauts may fly to Mars—or even farther into space.

On a mission lasting years, they will need to grow their own food.

In the ISS's laboratories, the crew is trying to grow vegetables.

So far, they've grown lettuce.

The crew ate some of the leaves and sent some back to Earth to be studied!

lettuce growing on the ISS

Like astronauts, plants are weightless in space. As plants grow, they can't tell which way is up or down. There's also no sunlight, rain, or soil inside a spacecraft.

Tiny Space Travelers

Everything on Earth is covered with germs and other **microbes**.

Scientists wanted to know how these **microscopic** living things might survive in space.

Samples of microbes were collected from dozens of places on Earth.

Then they were sent to the space station to be studied.

If these microbes are dangerous in space, it could affect the planning of future missions.

the *Tyrannosaurus rex* fossil

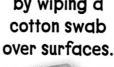

Samples were collected by wiping a cotton swab over surfaces.

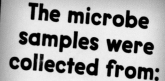

The microbe samples were collected from:

- A *Tyrannosaurus rex* fossil
- Sports stadiums
- The Liberty Bell
- The set of the *Today* show

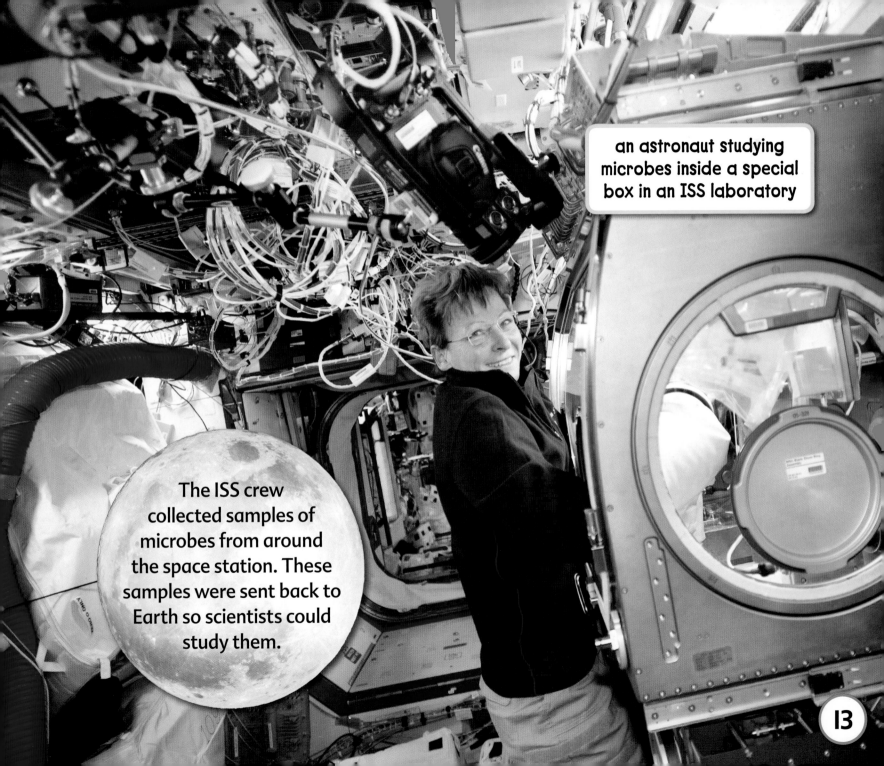

an astronaut studying microbes inside a special box in an ISS laboratory

The ISS crew collected samples of microbes from around the space station. These samples were sent back to Earth so scientists could study them.

Ready to Space Walk

One of the most dangerous jobs on the ISS is a space walk.

It takes about six hours to get ready.

First, an astronaut puts on special underwear in case he or she has to go to the bathroom.

Next, the astronaut climbs into a cooling suit that has cold water flowing through it.

Finally, he or she puts on a protective spacesuit and helmet.

an astronaut wearing a cooling suit

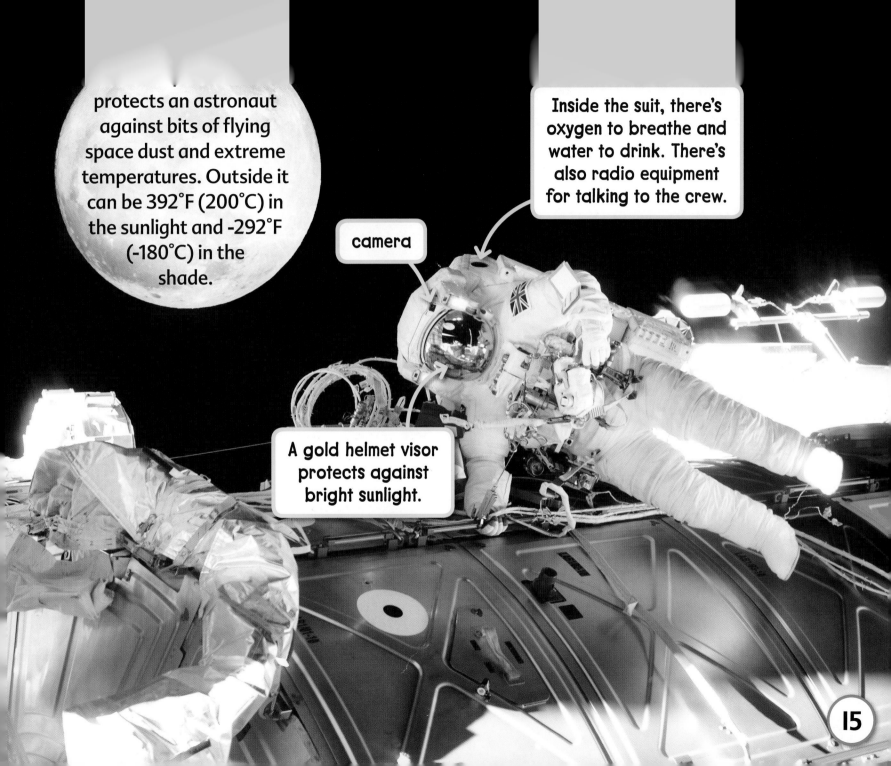

A Race Against Time

In January 2016, two astronauts performed a space walk.

Their mission was to replace some electronics on one of ISS's **solar arrays**.

Once in position, the men waited for Earth to block the Sun's light.

They had just 30 minutes before the sunlight returned and electricity surged through the array.

The brave astronauts successfully completed the repair!

an astronaut working on the solar arrays

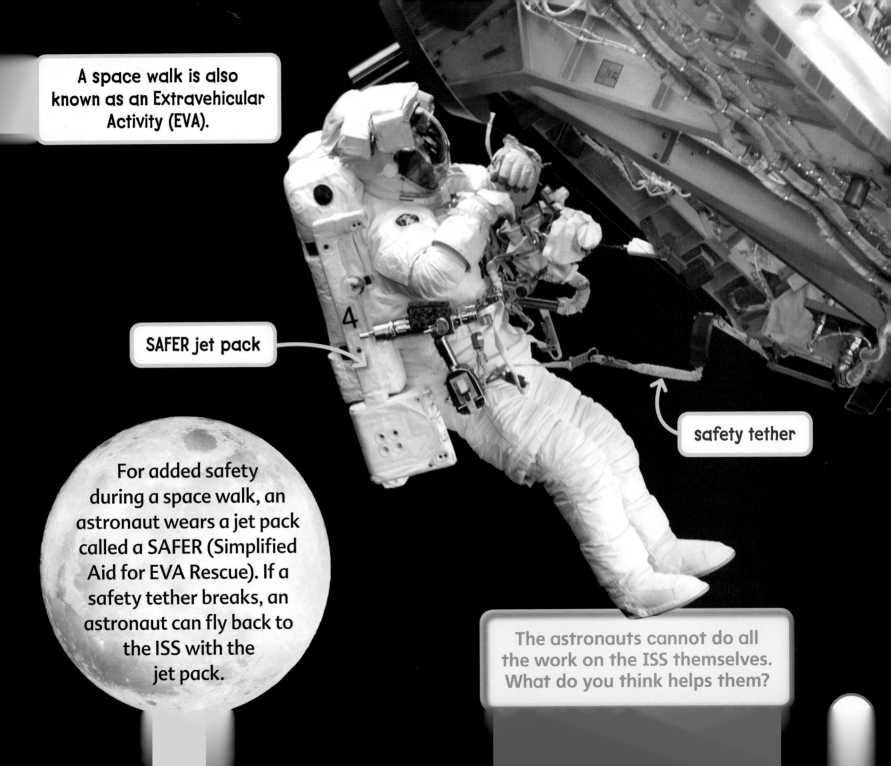

A space walk is also known as an Extravehicular Activity (EVA).

SAFER jet pack

safety tether

For added safety during a space walk, an astronaut wears a jet pack called a SAFER (Simplified Aid for EVA Rescue). If a safety tether breaks, an astronaut can fly back to the ISS with the jet pack.

The astronauts cannot do all the work on the ISS themselves. What do you think helps them?

The Robot Crew

The astronauts get help from robots!

The SPHERES are small, colorful robots.

They help with experiments about movement and weightlessness.

Astrobee is a robot that can make sure the air is safe to breathe.

It can even look for lost tools!

the SPHERES floating on the ISS

Astrobee has small fans that blow air to help it move around.

Astronaut Chores

Every morning, the ISS astronauts wake up, eat breakfast, and then get to work.

There are not only experiments to do—but lots of chores, too.

All waste, including astronaut poop, must be bagged up and blasted back to Earth.

When the day is over, the crew eats dinner, relaxes, and goes to sleep.

Then, it's time for another workday in space!

unpacking a delivery of fresh fruit

unblocking the space toilet

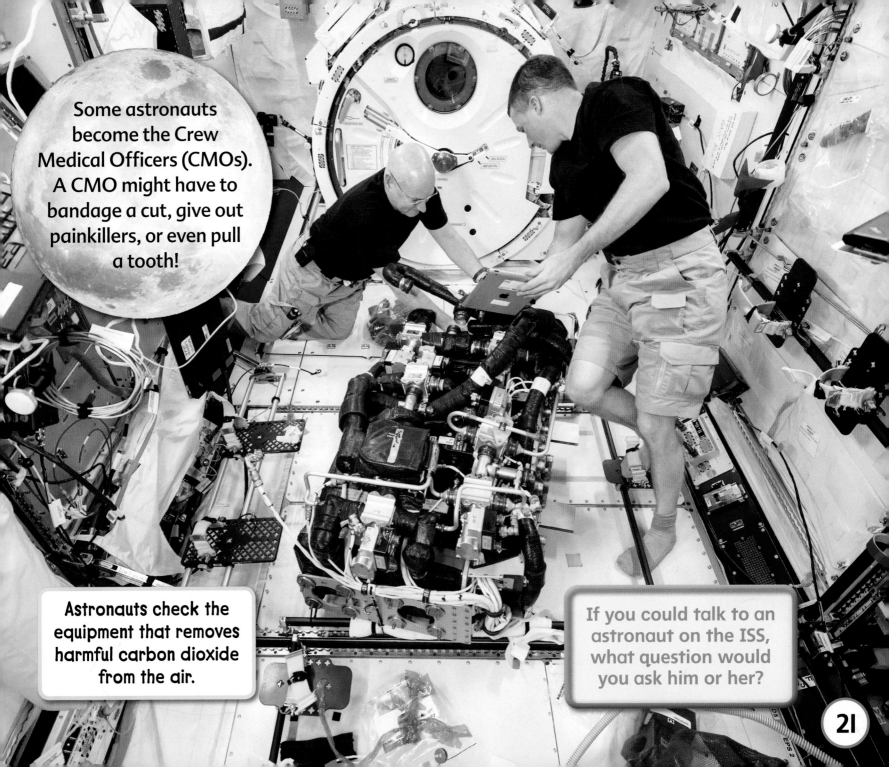

Some astronauts become the Crew Medical Officers (CMOs). A CMO might have to bandage a cut, give out painkillers, or even pull a tooth!

Astronauts check the equipment that removes harmful carbon dioxide from the air.

If you could talk to an astronaut on the ISS, what question would you ask him or her?

21

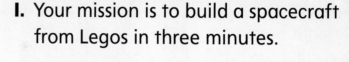

Science Lab

Working Like an Astronaut

During a space walk, astronauts must work quickly and carefully, and focus on multiple things at once. Try this test to see if you can work like an astronaut.

You will need:
- A selection of Lego pieces
- Thick gardening gloves
- A timer
- A friend to help you

I. Your mission is to build a spacecraft from Legos in three minutes.

2. You must wear thick gloves.

3. As you work, you must count backward from 100 to 0.

When you're ready to start, ask your helper to time you.

After you've completed the task, answer the following questions:

- *How did you feel during the task?*

- *Which part of the task did you find most difficult?*

- *In what ways do you think this test was like being on a space walk?*

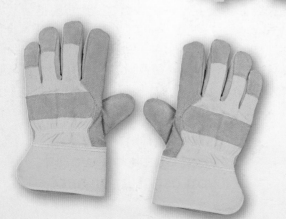

Science Words

laboratory (LA-bruh-tor-ee) a place where scientific experiments are carried out

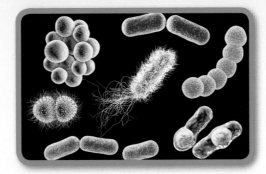

microbes (MYE-krohbs) tiny living things; some microbes cause disease

microscopic (mye-kroh-SKOP-ik) able to be seen only with a microscope

mission (MISH-uhn) a special job or task to be performed

orbiting (OR-bit-ING) circling, or moving around, another object

solar arrays (SOH-lur uh-RAYZ) panels that use the sun to produce electricity

Index

Read More

Gross, Miriam. *All About Space Stations (Blast Off!).* New York: Rosen (2009).

Morey, Allan. *The International Space Station (Space Tech).* Minnetonka, MN: Bellwether (2018).

Throp, Claire. *A Visit to a Space Station (Fantasy Science Field Trips).* North Mankato, MN: Heinemann-Raintree (2014).

Learn More Online

To learn more about working in space, visit
www.bearportpublishing.com/space-ology

About the Author

Ellen Lawrence lives in the United Kingdom and fully admits to being a huge space geek! While researching and writing this series, she loved watching interviews with astronauts and spine-tingling launch countdowns.

Answer for Page 5

Astronauts must be tethered, or connected, to the ISS to keep them from floating off into space. Astronauts also use tethers to keep tools from floating away.

24